Tommy's Tunes

A comprehensive collection of soldiers' songs, marching melodies, rude rhymes, and popular parodies, composed, collected, and arranged on Active Service with the B.E.F., by F. T. Nettleingham, 2nd Lt. R. F. C., and published by Erskine Macdonald, Ltd., London :: :: W.C. 1.

TOMMY'S TUNES

A COMPREHENSIVE COLLECTION OF SOLDIERS'
SONGS, MARCHING MELODIES, RUDE RHYMES,
AND POPULAR PARODIES, COMPOSED,
COLLECTED, AND ARRANGED ON ACTIVE
SERVICE WITH THE B. E. F., BY F. T.
NETTLEINGHAM, 2nd LT. R. F. C.

The Naval & Military Press Ltd

Published by

The Naval & Military Press Ltd
Unit 5 Riverside, Brambleside
Bellbrook Industrial Estate
Uckfield, East Sussex
TN22 1QQ England

Tel: +44 (0)1825 749494

www.naval-military-press.com
www.nmarchive.com

Printed and bound by CPI Group (UK) Ltd, Croydon, CR0 4YY

*In reprinting in facsimile from the original, any imperfections are inevitably reproduced
and the quality may fall short of modern type and cartographic standards.*

To
Ye that have sung,
Ye that have laughed,
Ye that were happy,
Amateurs at warcraft,
Amateurs all.

To
Ye that have cursed,
Ye that have prayed,
Ye that have joked,
And joking—were laid
Side by side.
Britons all.

Your songs were ribald,
Your rhymes were rude,
Your ditties doubtful,
Your quips quite crude,
But ye fought.
Heroes all.

1917.   F.T.N.

INDEX.

9

PARODIES INCLUDED.

PARODIES INCLUDED—*continued.*

NUMBERS OF SONGS IN WHICH THE FOLLOWING REGIMENTS ARE MENTIONED :—

Anzacs, Song No. 28.

Artists' Rifles, Song Nos. 22, 27.

A.S.C., Song Nos. 6, 15.

A.S.C., M.T., Song Nos. 25, 29.

Guards, Song No. 14.

Queen Victoria's Rifles, Song No. 56.

Royal Engineers, Sappers, Song Nos. 24, 33, 34, 86.

Royal Flying Corps, Song Nos. 1, 10, 26, 32, 38, 39, 61, 63, 64, 65, 67, 68, 69, 70, 71, 72, 73, 75, 76, 77, 78, 79, 80, 81, 82, 83.

Royal Fusiliers, Song No. 90.

R.N.A.S., Song No. 30.

R.N.D., Song 41.

Seaforth Highlanders, Song No. 86.

South Africans, Song No. 35.

INTRODUCTION.

I AM given to understand that some dear old ancient with a taste for biographies once exclaimed that, if he knew a people's songs, he could write their history. I'm content to leave it at that, though for the sake of those as dense and ignorant as myself, I would say that I suppose he meant that a nation's songs and other musical effort (and also literature) reveal the actual character and culture of a nation in a way that is unapproached by any other art or by rule of thumb.

Now, in the light of the following effusions, perpetrations—or even compositions, as some would wish them to be called—I shall leave severely alone such a controversial subject as Tommy's character, leaving it to my reviewers to thresh out by process of elimination!

My hitherto unspoken wish is that this collection of songs should be reviewed by none other than men with Army experience.

" By their words shall ye know them," or " By your words shall ye be judged," are parallel platitudes—yet think, indulgent reader, how far from accurate would be your judgment and idea of the British soldier were you to draw conclusions solely on his songs! You would picture a man—yea, an army, nowadays, even the nation—as lacking in *esprit de corps*, *armour propre*, discipline, or any other of those wise soldierly qualities

13

without which no collection of free people could stand the enormities of injustice and voluntary sacrifice which are demanded over an extended and sustained period by modern warfare. And you would be wrong! It is a peculiarity of British humour to be derogatory to its own dignity, to wipe itself in the mud, to affect self-satire to an alarming extent. Yet woe betide any foreigner who dares to opine we're not what we think we are. The spirit really evinced by these songs, in spite of their oft-times derogatory purport, is that of a lofty cynicism and a confirmed fatalism, but real, thick, unadulterated sarcasm—never.

Regarding the fatalistic tendency shown by Tommy in all his speech and actions, this will be noticed irrespective of his philosophy—Tommy may be Romanist, Protestant, Wesleyan, Atheist, Theosophist, or Agnostic, yet one and all betray the same traits and the same courage.

Although the great aim of this work is to present and perpetuate the original and unwritten tunes and rhymes, it must not be supposed that Tommy taboos any other sort. Of course, the latest music-hall ditties, with their swinging tunes, have a great vogue, but the enthusiasm soon wears off.

" Tipperary " was never greatly sung. I think it of interest to place on record how this song has actually stood in Tommy's estimation and in the favour of the world. Notwithstanding that it is now sung over five continents, and that our French friends—most of them —have Tipperary at their finger tips, and most of the street urchins and *parigots* sing it with equal exuberance in French and English—it was never Tommy's song.

George Curnock, *Daily Mail* representative at Boulogne when the first of the Expeditionary Force troops

14

arrived, heard some of them singing it ; new to him, as to most of us, he mentioned it in his report. The publishers naturally seized on such publicity and boomed for all it was worth a hitherto unknown and unwanted song of such mediocre worth that it was like any other of the hundred songs that appear and are sung by third-rate artistes, and then disappear ; the couplet of which, by the way, was a crib on " Has Anybody here seen Kelly." In other words, it merely " happened " that George Curnock heard " Tipperary " instead of another equally popular, which the same troops started up a few miles farther on.

Revenons à nos moutons, the Scotch have a reputation for lilting refrains, the Welsh for being musical enthusiasts and possessing good voices, but when all is weighed up, there is little to choose between a British crowd of soldiers from the three Kingdoms and Principality. The outstanding fact is that Scotch tunes (only the Scotties know their words) are the most popular and most often sung, and of them all, " Annie Laurie " has queen of place.

I have heard " Annie Laurie " in peace and war ; at home and abroad ; in camp and on the march ; in a big dining-hall with 300 men and no dinner, and for all time I think it will remain the greatest, most pathetic, soul-stirring refrain ever composed. When harmonised by a hundred or more men unconducted, yet sung with a tacit understanding of the necessities of musical light and shade, it remains embedded in one's memory for aye.

The only other tune that approaches it in popularity or has the same possibility is the harmonised version of " Home, Sweet Home." I lay great stress on the " harmonised version." In the first place, these songs and chanties are *always* harmonised, and I should judge that an average of one in five or six men can improvise a harmony easily—and all harmony in the Army is improvised. Most of the songs in this volume would be will-o'-the-wisp creations were it not for their harmonic rendering.

If a song is a success without harmony, you may be reasonably sure that it is a dirge or in a monotone style that fascinates by its sing-song tune to the extent of pleasing some and grating others; those whom it grates, however, have short shrift. It is immediately struck up for the discomfort of him who announced his displeasure thereat, and the dirge drawls on till everyone (metaphorically) reels under its (again metaphorically) anaesthetic influence.

In spite of enthusiasm for the new songs, the old, as I have just remarked, are by no means discarded. Harmonised choruses of " Ye Banks and Braes o' Bonnie Doon," " Genevieve," " Swanee River," " Dear Old Joe," " Kentucky Home," " The Bonnie Banks o' Loch Lomond," " White Wings," " Sweet Marie," " Clementine," " Beautiful Isle of the Sea," " Good Old Jeff," " Silver Threads among the Gold," " Killarney," " Kathleen Mavourneen," " Bonnie Mary," etc., etc., and harmonised versions of Tosti's " Good-bye," " Until," " The Rosary," " Where my Caravan has Rested," " There's a Long, Long Trail," " Somewhere a Voice is Calling," "A Perfect Day," are effective and pretty beyond words.

Although our soldiers do not have special tunes and words for special work and actions, as used our sailors with their chanties, or as have the Egyptian laborers to this day, Tommy is, nevertheless, a great singer. Certainly so in quantity if not in quality.

The rendering and the presentment may be—and usually is—crude, but surely we vie with our French allies in the innumerable swinging ditties that tradition and circumstance keep as unwritten heirlooms of our British Army and as souvenirs of forgotten wars.

Of course, it was Tommy of the old Armies and the Reservists who sang and whistled the most. The Territorials who had had camp holidays ran him close, but the New Army boys will now march for hours and miles in a weary, hang-dog fashion without striking any one of the scores of marching dirges that exist. Truly, the character of war has changed.

Soldiers' songs may be divided up into two classes : ROUTE AND MARCHING SONGS, CAMP OR CONCERT SONGS. These may again be subdivided into original and parodies. A further distinction could be made, though it is scarcely necessary, as regards the parodies ; in some cases both words and tunes have been lifted entire, and merely the nouns and adjectives altered, producing oft-times a bizarre effect and a violent change from pathos to bathos.

Under original, I think, must be included the adaptation of well-known tunes to original words, because the metre or measure coincides.

Apology must be made for the very amateurish way in which the special tunes are set down, without much regard for the rudiments of musical practice. I trust the public will understand the difficulty of collating and editing such a collection of songs on Active Service, and the still greater difficulty of putting the tunes to paper on Active Service by one who has no aptitude in that direction.

It will be noticed that well-known tunes or copyright

ones have been excluded, but all special or unique or compound tunes have been included. In some cases one tune is applied to three or four songs. One must rarely expect to find continuity of subject or even a connected sequence in a song of several verses. Many of the allusions are irrelevant one to the other.

In those songs of the concert type there is apparent a distinct desire to amuse, and although occasionally persons and institutions are sarcastically or caustically treated—local colour being invariably added—they contain actually no more harm than the topical allusions of a revue song.

In some cases the men take the opportunity for airing a grievance in some such diplomatic and unable-to-be-escaped-from manner. As a rule, leave, be it in England or Overseas, provides an omnipresent subject.

It is important to remember that local colour is added *ad lib*. Readers undoubtedly will find some verses to differ more or less extensively from the particular version known by them or sung in their crush.

These songs form a good dictionary as to Army vocabulary and argot. Such words or phrases as :

Pukkah	Proper, real ;
Wallah	A person, a foreigner (in a domestic sense) ;
Pozzi	Jam ;
Compris (pron. compree)	Understand—*not* understood—as it should be ;
Faché	Sorry, angry, cross ;
No bon	No good ;
Très bon!	Very good ;

Jig-a-jig	Love ;
Comme-ca !	Like that ;
Tout de suite (pron. *toot sweet*)	Immediately ;

are every hour terms with our soldiers in France and elsewhere, and annotation and references will be found where necessary, and have been retained by process of elimination.

It is a great pity that a large number of the wittiest—albeit, of a coarse kind—the gayest—as regards tune—and most frequently sung—therefore popular—creations are so untranslatable as to render them unprintable for general consumption, but as some of them have undoubtedly been in the Army for more than 100 years, it seems probable that they will remain unwritten heirlooms for an indefinite period, and in peace-time will be handed down through the generations by drummer-boy to drummer-boy.

Soldier readers of this work will appreciate to what extent I have purged some of their favourites, and will appreciate all the more the reason I found it impossible to present even a purged version of such songs as are mentioned in the next paragraph.

With such songs as " Miralto Me Re," " Kafoosalem, the harlot of Jerusalem," and " B. Bill the Sailor," it is worth placing on record for all time their titles, though I doubt very much whether their rhyming lines will ever find a rest in the British Museum.

I suppose I shall be inundated with new versions and totally new songs on the appearance of this volume, and I will earnestly ask all who intend telling me I've omitted their own regimental song to *also* forward the music or name of the tune, *if well known*, and they shall be included in the next edition, unless " there ain't going to be no next."

The large percentage of Aviation songs will be understood and condoned when it is remembered that the R.F.C. is the writers' corps, and also when gratitude is here expressed to the Editor of *Aeronautics* for permission to publish all such songs as have appeared in that excellent journal, and to whose prescience and encouragement the public are partly indebted for the present collection. My thanks are also due to the Editor of *Flying* for permission to publish such Flying Corps songs by me as have appeared lately in his journal. Please send me any new ones to make the collection more complete.

FREDK. THOS. NETTLEINGHAM,

2nd Lt. R.F.C.,

6 *Rue Christiania,*

Paris xviii.

1916-1917.

1. WHEN THIS RUDDY WAR IS OVER.*

The following is the particular version sung in the R.F.C. All these marching songs differ slightly, according to the Unit singing, a little local colour being invariably added.

When this ruddy war is over,
O ! how happy I shall be !
When this ruddy war is over
And we come back from Germany.
No more blooming kit inspection,
No more church parade for me.
When this ruddy war is over,
You can have your R.F.C.

When this ruddy war is over,
Oh ! how happy we shall be !
When this ruddy war is over
And we come back from Germany.
Roll on, when we go on furlough ;
Roll on, when we go on leave,
Then we'll catch the train for Blighty,
Though we'll leave the girls bereaved.

* A favourite with the " old soldier."

2. SKIBOO.

TUNE : Special.

Two German officers crossed the Rhine, Skiboo, Skiboo.
Two German officers crossed the Rhine, Skiboo, Skiboo.
   These German officers crossed the Rhine
   To love the women and taste the wine.
Skiboo, Skiboo, Skiboodley boo, Skidam, dam, dam.

They came to an inn on top of a rise, Skiboo, Skiboo,
A famous French inn of stupendous size, Skiboo, Skiboo,
   They saw a maiden all dimples and sighs,
   The two together said " Damn her eyes."
Skiboo, Skiboo, Skiboodley boo, Skidam, dam, dam.

Oh, landlord, you've a daughter fair, Skiboo, Skiboo,
Oh, landlord, you've a daughter fair, Skiboo, Skiboo.
   Oh, landlord, you've a daughter fair,
   With lily-white arms and golden hair.
Skiboo, Skiboo, Skiboodley boo, Skidam, dam, dam.

Nein, nein, mein Herr, she's far too young, Skiboo,
   Skiboo,
Nein, nein, mein Herr, she's far too young, Skiboo,
   Skiboo.
   Mais non, mon pere, I'm not so young—
   I've often been kissed by the farmer's son.
Skiboo, Skiboo, Skiboodley boo, Skidam, dam, dam.

SKIBOO—*cont.*

The rest of the tale I can't relate, Skiboo, Skiboo,
For tho' it's old, it's up to date, Skiboo, Skiboo.
  The story of man seducing a maid
  Is not for you—you're too sedate.
Skiboo, Skiboo, Skiboodley boo, Skidam, dam, dam.

A well-purged and diminutive version of a famous heirloom of the British Army ; in its original state consists of about forty verses.

3. TIPPERARY.

That's the wrong way to tickle Marie,
That's the wrong way to kiss :
Don't you know that over here, lad,
They like it better like this.
Hooray *pour la France !*
Farewell, *Angleterre !*
We didn't know the way to tickle Marie,
But now we've learnt how.

If ever you hear the air of Tipperary, it's almost certain they'll be singing the above. A little episode illustrating the fact that Tommy has made a conquest with the ladies of France in a way after their own heart.

4. THE LITTLE BIT OF FLUFF.*

TUNE : " *Tipperary.*"

It took a long time to get it hairy,.
  'Twas a long time to grow ;
Took a long time to get it hairy,
  For the toothbrush hairs to show.
Good-bye, Charlie Chaplin,
  Farewell, tufts of hair ;
'Twas a long, long time to get it hairy,
  But now my lip's quite bare.

* Popular about the time the W.O. rescinded its decision *re* moustaches.

5. SING ME TO SLEEP.
(TRENCH VERSION.)

Sing me to sleep where Very lights* fall,
Let me forget the war and all.
I've got the wind up,† that's what they say,
God strafe‡ 'em like hell—till break of day.
I feel so weary, warworn and sad,
I don't like this war—it makes me feel bad.
Dark is my dug-out—cold are my feet—§
Waiting for Boches to put me to sleep.

> Far, far from Wipers‖ I long to be,
> Where German snipers can't snipe at me.
> Take me to Egypt or Salonika,
> Where I can hear of the Boche¶ from afar.

Sing me to sleep where bullets fall,
Let me forget the war and all ;
Damp is my dug-out, cold are my feet,
Nothing but bully and biscuits to eat.
Sing me to sleep where bombs explode
And shrapnel shells are *à la mode* ;
Over the sandbags, helmets you'll find :
Corpses in front of you, corpses behind.

> Far from the starlights I'd love to be,
> Lights of old London I'd rather see ;
> Think of me crouching where worms creep,
> Waiting for someone to put me to sleep.

---

* A species of flare fired from a pistol, named after their inventor.
† To " have the wind up " is to have " cold feet " ; afraid, nervy.
‡ To punish—a by now permanent word in the English language.
§ Another reference to fear which might also have a more literal significance.
‖ " Wipers " refers to Ypres, also called Epray.
¶ German.

As a point of interest I will give to the uninitiated other instances of current war phraseology :—

" HOT AIR."—Much ado about nothing ; to have plenty of

6. DIVISIONAL REST.*

TUNE : Special.

So when we came up for the first time
We had such a pain in our chest.
We'd had umpteen† drills and inspections,
And they called it Divisional Rest.

And when we came up for the second time,
Captain Tickler and A.S.C. men
Had been sending home their old horseshoes
To thicken his father's Jam.

And when we came up for the third time,
We were told there was something anew :
All the cooks in the company
Could cook something else than stew.

And when we came up for the fourth time,
We said, " Strike me pink, Gawd blimey " :
We were told a Colonial soldier
Had saluted the G.O.C.‡

SING ME TO SLEEP—*continued.*

go ; to be officious ; to give instructions which others consider superfluous, or are disinclined to carry out.

" EYEWASH."—Originated owing to " Eyewitness " stories or despatches at the beginning of the war ; applied to most circular memoranda received, particularly about wearing of slacks or Sam Brownes, saluting, or economisation of petrol ; something to be winked at.

" SWINGING THE LEAD."—To swing the lead is to malinger or to feign—thus, a lead swinger is really a malingerer or a shirker ; to be sent on a job and not do it is to " swing the lead." When in hospital, to make one's ailments or wounds more serious than they really are is to " swing the lead " on the Doctor. Needless to add, it bears no relation to that other vulgar metaphor—"to throw one's weight about " !

" HOT-STUFFED."—Stolen. *To hotstuff* — to steal, pinch, lift, or to appropriate by other than rightful procedure. *A hotstuffer*—one who steals.

DIVISIONAL REST.

* When regiments are withdrawn from the line.
† Any number, too numerous to count.
‡ Refers to slackness in saluting by Colonial soldiers.

7. GROUSING.

Tune: " *Holy, Holy, Holy.*"

Grousing, Grousing, Grousing,
Always blooming well grousing.
Roll on till my time is up,
And I shall grouse no more.
Grousing, Grousing, Grousing,
Always blooming well grousing.
Roll on till my time is up,
And I shall grouse no more.

Raining, Raining, Raining,
Always bally well raining.
Raining all the morning,
And raining all the night.
Raining, Raining, Raining,
Always bally well raining.
Roll on till my time is up,
And I shall grouse no more.

Marching, Marching, Marching,*
Always ruddy well marching.
Marching all the morning,
And marching all the night.
Marching, Marching, Marching,
Always ruddy well marching.
Roll on till my time is up,
And I shall march no more.

---

* I have heard of this being sternly suppressed by company commanders, where men have spent long hours on the march, as being detrimental to good discipline.

8. ODE TO TICKLER.*

TUNE: "*Sweet Genevieve.*"

Oh, jam for tea! Oh, jam for tea,
I'm jolly sure it don't suit me;
I've tried for years, and now in tears,
I'll sing it to you mournfully.

Oh, jam for tea! Oh, jam for tea!
The world knows how you've tortured me;
I've frills and squills, you've made me bills,
And filled the dentists' empty tills.

Oh, jam for tea! Oh, jam for tea!
Fried bully† and Maconochie;‡
But when we get back to Blighte-e-e-e....
We will have ham and lamb for tea.

* Jam maker to the Army.
† Bully beef—otherwise corned beef.
‡ The maker's name: a tinned food issued to Tommy, consisting usually of tinned tomatoes, haricots, potatoes, some sort of meat, usually fat, and some shiny stuff that might be gravy or jelly.

9. THE REASON WHY.

TUNE: "*Auld Lang Syne.*"

We're here because we're here,
Because we're here Because we're here.
We're here because we're here,
Because we're here, Because we're here.
Oh, here we are, oh, here we are,
Oh, here we are again.
Oh, here we are, oh, here we are,
Oh, here we are again.

AND SO ON, until exhausted.

27

10. NEVER MIND.*

(NEW VERSION.)

Though your heart may ache awhile, never mind,
Though your heart may ache awhile, never mind,
    You'll forget about it soon,
    When you've had a good old spoon,
And your heart, it aches no more, never mind.

If the Sergeant's pinched your rum—never mind,
If the Sergeant's on the bum†—never mind.
If he collars all your fags, and you've nothing on but rags,
It's his affair—not yours—so never mind.

If the Sergeant says your daft—never mind.
Maybe you are—who knows ?—never mind.
It's no use to answer back, 'cos he won't stand any slack,‡
So if he says you're daft—then you are.

The following has reference to a certain R.F.C. sergeant, who went to fetch rations in a sidecar, the light tender usually employed for this purpose being otherwise engaged. Not being able to get it all in, he tied the bread round the side and back. When he arrived at the unit, not unnaturally the bread was "napoo."§

At lunch-time you might have heard a serenade to the following effect :

If the Sergeant's lost your bread—never mind.

If he sticks it round a side car—never mind.

And even if it's messed—he did it for the best,

For he's the Sergeant—dontcherknow—so never mind.

* This song, with its many verses, shows Tommy as a confirmed fatalist.
  † On the borrow.
  ‡ Cheek.
  § " Napoo "—Tommy's version of " *Il n'y-a plus* ; " used in divers senses, usually to say : no more ; not there ; gone. Used in the same sense as *Vamoosed*.

11. OUR LITTLE WET TRENCH IN THE WEST.

TUNE: " *Little Grey Home in the West.*"

In a little wet trench in the west,
Where the Germans cannot get at me,
It's not very grand, and we most of us stand,
And the only good thing is our tea.
Over there where the great big shells fall,
The Huns are afraid of us—lest
We should bayonet them with true British phlegm,
Should they visit our home in the west.

There are hands that will welcome them out,
There are guns that are waiting to fire,
There are eyes that look out for a chance of a bout,
Though we're up to our eyes in the mire.
It's a hell upon earth for us all,
But we mean to be first on the ball.
When the kick-off takes place, we'll be first in the race,
From our little wet trench in the west

There are dug-outs and other things new,
Funk-holes, trench mortars, bombs and grenades,
The only thing hot is our ration of stew,
Don't we we wish we were back at our trades ?
Never mind—we're out on the job,
Though we're not paid at Union Rates,
Oh ! we shan't rest content till we've made a big dent
In another wet trench in the west.

FLANDERS, 1914.

12. APRÈS LA GUERRE.

Après la guerre fini,
Oh, we'll go home to Blighty ;
But won't we be sorry to leave chère Germaine,
Après la guerre fini.

Après la guerre fini,
English soldier parti,
Mam'selle français beaucoup picanninies,
Après la guerre fini.

This song, which has several more verses, is a great favourite. Its original air is " Sous les Ponts de Paris." The pidgin French is typical of the way Tommy and the natives converse. I blush to say that Tommy sings this at his best when passing through a small village, where, unhappily, its truth is only too apparent, though, naturally, it is not necessary or possible to wait for the end of the war, as the words indicate.

The curious and pathetic part in most cases is that mothers are not always certain whether these war babies are French, English, or even German. Time is inexorable, but blood will out—*on verra.*

13. AT THE HALT, ON THE LEFT, FORM PLATOON.

TUNE : " *Red, White and Blue.*"

At the halt, on the left, form platoon.
At the halt, on the left, form platoon.
If the odd numbers don't mark time two paces,
How the hell can the rest form platoon ?

14. LA-LA, LA-LA.

TUNE: "*La-la, La-la, sing this Chorus to me.*"

La-la, La-la, there's going to be some fun,
La-la, La-la, Tommy's got his gun.
When he gets at the end of it,
He won't forget to shoot and hit.
La-la, La-la, the Hun is on the run.
One, two, three—it fills us with delight
To see the Boches fall.
Four, five, six—with all your main and might,
We're going to shift the Hun from off the ball.

La-la, La-la, there's going to be some fun,
La-la, La-la, the Boche is on the run.
When he sees the steel and bit,
He promptly hides and has a fit.
La-la, La-la, we've got them on the run.
Seven, eight, nine, it fills us with delight
To see the Boches fall.
Ten, eleven, twelve, you should see them dig and delve,
We're just spoiling for a brawl.

La-la, La-la, this will not be fun,
La-la, La-la, we're running short of rum.
When we get to the end of it,
We shan't forget to grouse a bit.
La-la, La-la, we shall blame the sergeant some.
Now, mark my word, it fills us with delight
To drink our tot of rum.
Hurrah! Hurrah! Hurrah! we'll all get tight
The day that rum does come.

THE GUARDS (Ypres, 1914).

15. OLD KING COLE.

(A.S.C. Version.)

Old King Cole was a merry old soul
And a merry old soul was he,
He called for his pipe and called for his bowl
And he called for his Privates three.

> Now every private had a great thirst,
> And a very great thirst had he,
> "Beer! Beer!! Beer!!! Beer!!!!" said the privates,
> Very merry men are we,
> For there's none so fair as can compare
> With the boys of the A.S.C.

Old King Cole was a merry old soul,
And a merry old soul was he,
He called for his pipe and he called for his bowl
And he called for his Sergeants three.

> Now every sergeant had a loud voice,
> And a very loud voice had he,
> " Move to the right in fours," said the sergeants,
> " Beer! Beer!! Beer!!! Beer!!!!" said the privates,
> " Very merry men are we,
> For there's none so fair as can compare
> With the boys of the A.S.C."

Old King Cole was a merry old soul,
And a merry old soul was he,
He called for his pipe and he called for his bowl
And he called for his Subalterns three.

> Now every subaltern had a big grouse,
> And a very big grouse had he.
> " We do all the work," said the subalterns,
> " Move to the right in fours," said the sergeants,

"Beer! Beer! ! Beer! ! ! Beer! ! ! !" said the privates,
"Very merry men are we,
For there's none so fair as can compare
With the boys of the A.S.C."

Old King Cole was a merry old soul,
And a merry old soul was he,
He called for his pipe and he called for his bowl
And he called for his Captains three.

Now every captain had a fine figure,
And a very fine figure had he,
"We want three months' leave," said the captains,
"We do all the work," said the subalterns,"
"Move to the right in fours,' said the sergeants,
"Beer! Beer! ! Beer! ! ! Beer! ! ! !" said the privates,
"Very merry men are we,
For there's none so fair as can compare
With the boys of the A.S.C."

Old King Cole was a merry old soul,
And a merry old soul was he,
He called for his pipe and he called for his bowl
And he called for his adjutants three.

Now every adjutant had a pair of fine spurs,
A pair of very fine spurs had he.
"Where the hell's my horse?" said the adjutant,
"We want three months' leave," said the captains,
"We do all the work," said the subalterns,
"Move to the right in fours," said the sergeants,
"Beer! Beer! ! Beer! ! ! Beer! ! ! !" said the privates,
"Very merry men are we,
For there's none so fair as can compare
With the boys of the A.S.C."

Old King Cole was a merry old soul,
And a merry old soul was he,
He called for his pipe and he called for his bowl
And he called for his Majors three.

> Now every major had a big swear,
> And a very big swear had he.
> " Blankety, Blankety, Blank," said the major,
> " Where the hell's my horse," said the adjutant,
> " We want three months' leave," said the captains,
> " We do all the work," said the subalterns,
> " Move to the right in fours," said the sergeants,
> " Beer ! Beer ! ! Beer ! ! ! Beer ! ! ! ! " said the privates,
> " Very merry men are we,
> For there's none so fair as can compare
> With the boys of the A.S.C."

Old King Cole was a merry old soul,
And a merry old soul was he,
He called for his pipe and he called for his bowl
And he called for his Colonels three.

> Now every Colonel had a sore head,
> And a very sore head had he.
> " What's the next word of command ? " said the
>   Colonel,
> " Blankety, Blankety, Blank," said the major,
> " Where the hell's my horse ? " said the adjutant,
> " We want three months' leave," said the captains,
> " We do all the work," said the subalterns,
> " Move to the right in fours," said the sergeants,
> " Beer ! Beer ! ! Beer ! ! ! Beer ! ! ! ! " said the privates,
> " Very merry men are we,
> " For there's none so fair as can compare
> With the boys of the A.S.C."

Old King Cole was a merry old soul,
And a merry old soul was he,
He called for his pipe and he called for his bowl
And he called for his Generals three.

> Now every general had two red tabs,
> And two red tabs had he.
> " What's the plan of campaign ? " said the general,
> " What's the next word of command ? " said the
>   colonel,
> " Blankety, Blankety, Blank," said the major,
> " Where the hell's my horse ? " said the adjutant,
> " We want three months' leave," said the captains,
> " We do all the work," said the subalterns,
> " Move to the right in fours," said the sergeants,
> " Beer ! Beer ! ! Beer ! ! ! Beer ! ! ! ! " said the privates,
> " Very merry men are we,
> For there's none so fair as can compare
> With the boys of the A.S.C."

16. SWANEE RIVER.

(PARIS VERSION.)

Walking up and down the Champs Elysees,*
        That's what we like ;
Oh ! you should see *la femme*—how she eyes us
With " boko " † admiration ‡—so says Mike.
> If the war is sad and dreary,
> Nought we know of that ;
> We all know a *demoiselle* so *cherie*,
> Also her charming little flat.

* To be pronounced as in English.
† *Beaucoup*—much.
‡ Pronounce as in French.

17. SHE WAS SO KIND TO ME.

Tune : Special.

She was so good and so kind to me
And all the rest of the family ;
She was so good and so kind to me,
She was, she was, she was. ......
.... So good and so kind to me, etc.

18. WHY DID WE JOIN THE ARMY ?

Tune : " *Here's to the Maiden of Sweet Seventeen*" and " *Fol-the-Rol-Lol.*"

Why did we join the Army, boys ?
Why did we join the Army ?
Why did we come to Salisbury Plain ?—
We must have been ruddy well balmy.
  Fol-the-rol-lol, fol-the-rol-lol,
  Fol-the-rol-lol, me laddie ;
  Fol-the-rol-lol, fol-the-rol-lol,
  Fol-the-rol-lol, me laddie.

19. I DON'T WANT TO BE A SOLDIER.

TUNE : " *Come, my lad, and be a Soldier.*"

I don't want to be a soldier,
I don't want to go to war ;
    I'd rather roam
    Here at home,
And keep myself on the earnings of a lady typist.
I don't want a bayonet in my stomach,
Nor my eyelids shot away,
    For I am quite happy
    With my mammy and my pappy—
So I wouldn't be a soldier any day.

20. RECRUITING PARODY No. 2.

TUNE : " *Your King and Country Need You.*"

For we don't want your loving,
And we think you're awfully slow
To see that we don't want you,
So, please, won't you go.
We don't like your sing-songs,
And we loathe your refrain,
So don't you dare to sing it
Near us again.

Now, we don't want to hurry you,
But it's time you ought to go ;
For your songs and your speeches
They bore us so.
Your coaxings and pettings
Drive us nigh insane :
Oh ! we hate you, and'll boo you and hiss you
If you sing it again.

A typical parody on the recruiting songs, with which the soldiers—and slackers *and* everyone else—were soon fed up.
See also " *Your King and Country need you.*"

21. TIPS.

TUNE : *" Ragtime Cowboy Joe."*

When you've landed in the country,
    And you're fed up with the train,
Don't think your troubles finished,
    For they will follow in a chain ;
So keep your faces smiling
    When the billet meets your eye,
You all expected different,
    But to sleep you'll surely try.
When reveille breaks your slumber,
    To wash your thoughts will jump ;
But no blessed water can you get,
    There's no handle on the pump.
But streams there are in plenty,
    So your Christian ways redeem ;
But take care you don't fall in one—
    Things are not always what they seem.
If the language you go in for,
    It will play you funny pranks,
But the language most convincing
    Is the colour of five francs.
Then you patronise Estaminets,
    And you learn to drink the beer,
It has redeeming features,
    For it never makes you queer.
You will try to Parley-voo,
    With one and all you see,
And you get some nasty shocks,
    When they tell you : " Me no comprée."*
So you drop back on good old English,
    And swear like a Spanish Don,

Then smack your lips o'er the beer you drink,
    And say this, " Tres Bon."
When with rats and lice tormented,
    For the trenches you declare,
Don't think your troubles left behind,
    They'll follow everywhere.
So like the old Crusader,
    With a helmet on your head,
You march in full equipment,
    And wish the Kaiser dead.
On arrival in the trenches,
    Just keep your head down tight,
And remember that to show yourself
    Is asking for " Good-night."
When home no doubt you grumbled,
    If they hadn't made your bed,
But you'll be lucky in the dug-out
    To find a place to rest your head.
When walking through the trenches,
    You off the boards do slip ;
Don't pretend you did it purposely,
    As you dearly loved a dip.
When you're out upon patrol work,
    And a flare lights up the sky,
Be sure to lie quite flat and still,
    Or for you young Fritz will try.
When you cook upon the brazier,
    And your pals come round to talk,
Don't let the captain catch you
    Using bayonet as toasting fork.
Your helmet, too, was issued
    From shrapnel fire to save you,

39

TIPS—*cont.*

So don't think it is a saucepan,
  To be used for making " Gippo."†
When worn out with making gooseberries,
  And you wish it all in ——,
Don't curse the Sergt.-Major,
  If " Stand to " he has to yell.
Just the same with all your rations.
  When the bread is rather bare,
Don't curse the Quartermaster ;
  Some day you'll have your share.
And when back again in billets,
  Although people may prove kind,
You'll ne'er see a damsel half so nice
  As the one you left behind.

---

* This is not the natives' pidgin English or Tommy's pidgin French, but a real sample of the atrocious French spoken by some of the peasants and villagers with whom our troops find themselves ; also, it is not *patois*—that they speak fluently. " Me no allez " is also often heard. No grammar exists in the French of these people. You will often be addressed as follows : " Vois la la-bas boutique no bon l'autre tres bon, mademoiselle tres jolie."

† Soup, *ragout.*

Gippo, which comes from the Arabic, is merely one of many such words incorporated in Army parlance by the British Army' long association with the Orient. *Pozzi*—jam ; *wallah*—as person ; *pukkah*—proper, real, genuine, are a few of the commonest.

In this parody, as usual, the Sergeant-Major, food and girls form good topics for a rhyme.

22. RULE, BRITANNIA.

Rule, Britannia, Britannia rules the waves,
Britons never, never, never shall be
M-a-r-r-i-e-d to a mermaid at the bottom of the deep
    blue sea.

          Hoch ! Hoch ! mein Gott !
          What a damned fine lot
          Are the Artists' O.T.C.

This, as will be seen, is a mad medley of three tunes.

23. ONE MORE RIVER.

TUNE : Special.

One more river,
One more river to Jordan ;
One more river,
One more river to cross.

    The animals went in two by two,
    One more river to cross ;
    The elephant and the kangaroo,
    One more river to cross.

One more river,
One more river to Jordan ;
One more river,
One more river to cross.

          ETC., ETC.

24. FRED KARNO'S ARMY.
(R.E. VERSION.)
TUNE : " *The Church's One Foundation.*"

We are Fred Karno's Army,
A jolly fine lot are we :
Fred Karno is our Captain,
Charlie Chaplin our O.C.
And when we get to Berlin,
The Kaiser he will say :
Hoch ! Hoch ! mein Gott !
What a jolly fine lot
Are the 2-4th R.E., T.

25. KITCHENER'S ARMY.
(A.S.C., M.T. VERSION.)
TUNE : " *The Church's One Foundation.*"

Oh ! we're in Kitchener's Army,
We are the A.S.C.
We cannot fight, we cannot shoot,
So what earthly use are we ?
And when we get to Berlin,
The Kaiser he will say :
" Hoch ! Hoch ! mein Gott !
What a blooming fine lot
To draw six bob a day.

26. THE RAGTIME ARMY.
TUNE : " *The Church's One Foundation.*"

We are the Ragtime Army,
We are the R.F.C.
We do not fight, we cannot fly,
So what earthly use are we ?
And when we get to Berlin
The Kaiser he will say,
" Hoch ! Hoch ! mein Gott !
What a blooming fine lot
Are the boys of the R.F.C."

27. WE ARE THE RAGTIME ARMY.

TUNE: "*The Church's One Foundation.*"

We are the Ragtime Army,
The Artists' O.T.C.
We cannot drill, we cannot shoot,
What earthly use are we?
And when we've got to Berlin
The Kaiser he will say:
"Hoch! Hoch! mein Gott!
What a damned fine lot
Are the Artists' O.T.C."

28. ANZAC VERSION.

TUNE: "*The Church's One Foundation.*"

We are the Ragtime Army,
The A.N.Z.A.C.'s,
We do not shoot, we won't salute,
What bally use are we?
And when we get to Berlin,
The Kaiser he will say:
Hoch! Hoch! mein Gott!
What a fine jolly lot
Are the A.N.Z.A.C.'s.

We are the only heroes
Who stormed the Dardanelles,
And when we get to Berlin
They'll say, "What bally sells."
You boast and spite from morn till night
And think you're very brave,
But the men who really did the job
Are dead and in their graves.

29. ALLEY SLOPER'S CAVALREE.

TUNE: "*The Church's One Foundation.*"

We are the Mechanical Transport,
The M.T., A.S.C.,
We cannot march, we cannot fight,
What earthly good are we ?
And when we get to Berlin,
The Kaiser, he will say,
" Hoch ! Hoch ! mein Gott !
What a blooming rotten lot
Ally Sloper's Cavalree.*

We are the Mechanical Transport,
The Empty Cavalree,
We never march, we never fight,
What earthly use are we ?
And when we get to Berlin,
Old Kaiser Bill will say,
Hoch ! Hoch ! mein Gott !
What a —— rotten lot
To get six bob a day.†

* Derived from the initial letters of A.S.C.
† Refers to men specially enlisted on outbreak of war, who get six shillings a day.

30. THE RAGTIME NAVY.

TUNE: "*The Church's One Foundation.*"

We are the Ragtime Navy,
R.N.A.S. are we.
We cannot fight, we cannot shoot,
What b—— good are we ?
And when we get to Berlin,
The Kaiser he will say :
Hoch ! Hoch ! mein Gott !
What a b—— fine lot
To earn four bob a day.

31. THE WAIL OF THE NEW ARMIES.

TUNE : " *There is a Happy Land.*"

Where are our uniforms ?
Far, far away.
When will our rifles come ?
P'raps, pr'aps some day.
And you bet we shan't be long
Before we're fit and strong,
You'll hear us say, " *Oui, oui, tres bong.*"
When we're far away.

32. THIS IS THE FLYING CORPS.

TUNE : " *There is a Happy Land.*"

This is the Flying Corps,
So people say,
Where air mechanics lay the drains
For two bob a day.
Oh ! you should hear them sing,
" Roll on when my four* is in,
Then back home my hook I'll sling,
And there I'll stay.

* Refers to men enlisted for four years or four years in
the reserve.

33. WE ARE THE ROYAL SAPPERS.

TUNE : " *We are but Little Children Weak.*"

We are the Royal Sappers, we,
We only earn five bob a week.
The more we work
The more we may—
It makes no difference to our pay.

34. GINGER IS AN ENEMY OF MINE.

TUNE : Special.

He's an enemy of mine,
He's an enemy of mine :
We haven't seen old Ginger
For quite a hell of a time.
Just like a bee,
Always on the bumble,
Up and down the line
To see what he can rumble.
We haven't seen old Ginger
For umpteen blooming years,
For Ginger is a major in the Royal Engineers.

35. D'YE KEN JAN SMUTS?

TUNE: " *John Peel.*"

D'ye ken Jan Smuts when he's out with his gun,
D'ye ken Jan Smuts with his foes on the run,
D'ye ken Jan Smuts when he's hunting the Hun,
With his Horse and his Foot in the morning?

CHORUS:

  For the Kaiser he started the whole bloomin' war,
  So we'll strafe old Bill till he swanks no more,
  And the King shall be boss where the Hun was before,
  When we haul up the flag in the morning.

And I'll follow Jan Smuts wheresoever I am,
For the swamp and the jungle I don't care a damn,
From Kilimanjaro to Dar-es-Salaam,
Till we haul up the flag in the morning.

So here's to Jan Smuts, with three British cheers,
We wouldn't half smile if the toast was in Beers.
But mind that no bloomin' old submarine hears,
Or we'll wake up in heaven in the morning.

A popular parody sung on transports proceeding to German East Africa.

36. HIAWATHA.

(GALLIPOLI VERSION.)

When the moon shines bright on Charlie Chaplin,
          He's going balmy
          To join the Army;
And his old baggy trousers want a-mending
          Before they send him
          To the Dardanelles.

It will be noticed that Mr. Chaplin is a frequently mentioned individual, in one case attaining the dignity of a C.O.

37. A TRENCH PARODY.

TUNE : " *My Old Kentucky Home.*"

I've lost my Lattey sight !
Can't fire a shot at night !
There's something scaring me ;
Through all my plates I see
A German snipers' post
Ten yards away at most !
Boche rifles sticking through
From every point of view !

CHORUS 1.

I've a windy feeling round my heart
And I want to burrow down,
To get my gun and have a run
To dear old London town.
You can keep your sniperscopes—
Just give me telescopes
Pushed through grasses,
And my glasses.
But I'm frightened to death to know
That I must stay right here,
For I badly want to stroll,
For it seems to me
'Tain't no jubilee
In this sanguinary hole.

CHORUS 2.

I've a joyful feeling round my heart,
For the Boche has fallen down !
I'll shut my plate or I'll be late
For dear old London town.
You can keep your sniperscope :
Just give me one good hope

Of boat and Blighty ;
No more fighty—
I'll be tickled to death to know
That when I once get there
I can chuck my pack away !
Come along, you boys,
Make a deuce of a noise,
Fill a bumper to " The Day."

38. OMER DROME.*

TUNE : " *My Old Kentucky Home.*"

I've got a windy feeling round my heart
  And it's time that we went home,
I've got a great big longing to depart
  Somewhere back to Omer Drome.
Huns are diving at my tail,
Wind up—Gee !—I've got a gale.
  Guns are jamming,†
  Pilots damning,‡
Archies§ bursting all around us.
  And observers say,
" Ain't it time that we came down."
  So won't you splitass‖ back
  Along the track
To my dear old OMER TOWN.

* St. Omer.
† A frequent occurrence.
‡ A more frequent occurrence.
§ Anti-aircraft guns.
‖ Stunt flying, or in a reckless manner. The expression " a splitass merchant " is applied indiscriminately to a reckless individual or to a really good flyer capable of executing stunts with a modicum of safety.

39. THEY WERE HAPPY, OH! SO HAPPY.

Tune: *" Back Home in Tennessee."*

They were happy, Oh! so happy
When they left Germany
To fly across the sea—
No danger did they see.
The men and guns were ready for the Huns
When they got to Cuffley Town.
And what a light and what a sight
When we brought it to the ground.

Chorus :

Their home in Germany,
That Zepp will never see.
Count Zeppelin on his knees,
He thought the world of these.
All he could think of that night
Were the searchlights shining bright.
Guns were whizzing—crowds were hissing—
That Zepp was soon alight.
The people at their doors then shouted
out encores
When an airman brought it down
In a field near Enfield Town.
We'd been prepared to meet it,
Just imagine how we cheered it,
When it came down,
When it came down,
To its doom near London Town.

For the station crowds were making,
All a merry band.
They all thought it was grand,
They shook Robinson's hand.

The King soon heard and he sent word
The V.C. he had won.
And we're all glad and proud of the lad,
For his duty he has done.

CHORUS :

Their home in Germany, etc.

Written and composed by Ptes. SUNDERLAND and FLEET,
A.S.C., M.T.

40. OUR ESSEX CAMP.

TUNE : " *Back Home in Tennessee.*"

Down in our Essex camp,
That's where we get the cramp
Through sleeping in the damp ;
We're not allowed a lamp.
All we get there each day
Is left, right, left, right, all the way ;
Sergeants calling, lance-jacks* bawling
" Get out on parade."
We go to bed at night,
You ought to see the sight,
The earwigs on the floors
All night are forming fours.
If we're in bed in the morning,
You will hear the sergeant yawning :
" Show a leg there, show a leg there,"
'Way down in our Essex camp.

* Lance-corporals.

41. THE GALLANT R.N.D.*

Tune: *"John Brown's Baby."*

Im going to sing a song about the gallant R.N.D.,
The lads who're in the Army though they ought to be
   at sea;
Wherever they may send us matters nought to you or me,
   We'll just go marching along.

Chorus:
   Why don't they send us back to Blighty?
   Why don't they send us back to Blighty?
   Why don't they send us back to Blighty?
   For they don't want the R.N.D.

We've got some lovely washhouses with water taps galore,
There's a trough right down the middle, and there's
   basins by the score,
We can always get a decent wash—if we turn out at four,
   So we all turn out at four.

Three times a day the bugle sounds the ever-welcome
   call,
One by one we march into the great big dining hall,
We always get a dinner, and although it may be small,
   Gott strafe maconochie! †

When you want to see the doctor, you're not feeling
   very fine,
Maybe it's your liver got entangled with your spine,
You're asked the usual questions and given a number
   nine,‡
   Then back to work you go.

We've got a recreation ground where we go out to play,
The bull ring is the name of it ; we go there every day ;
We practise killing Germans, they're though only stuffed
    with hay,
    With the long point, short point—jab !

When we dodge the bull ring we are marching to and fro,
Sloping arms by numbers we've forgotten long ago,
Instead of teaching us the things we really ought to know,
    As a sentry we will stand at ease.

We have a kit inspection§ when there's nothing else to do,
You get a grand court-martial if you lose your four by
    two,¶
For the people at the War Office they seem to take the
    view
    That that's the way to win the war.

We never do a grumble now, wherever we are sent,
Though I'd sooner be in bed than sleeping fifteen in
    a tent ;‖
Of course we could take thirty men if they were slightly
    bent,
    And pile them on two deep.

* Royal Naval Division.
† The maker's name of a tinned concoction consisting of
meat, potatoes, beans, tomatoes, parsnips, and various other
things—makes a pretty sort of Irish stew. Variously pronounced
mac-onoch-*y*, or more often ma-*cono-chy*.
‡ A pill given as opening medicine ; a cure for all ills.
§ Tommy's bane, as mentioned elsewhere.
¶ Calico 4 ins. by 2 ins., used as a " pull through " for cleaning
the bores of rifles, etc.
‖ Twelve to 15 men in a tent is only too common.

42. THE GRASSHOPPER.

TUNE: "*John Brown's Body.*"

One grasshopper jumped right over another grasshopper's back,
And another grasshopper jumped right over the other
grasshopper's back,
A third grasshopper jumped right over the two grass
hoppers' backs,
Whilst a fourth grasshopper jumped over all the other
grasshoppers' backs.

We were only playing leapfrog,
We were only playing leapfrog,
We were only playing leapfrog,
Whilst the other grasshopper jumped right over the
other grasshopper's back.

43. JOHN BROWN'S BABY.
TUNE: "*John Brown's Body.*"

John Brown's baby's got a pimple on his—sh'sh !
John Brown's baby's got a pimple on his—sh'sh !
John Brown's baby's got a pimple on his—sh'sh !
And we all went marching home.
Glory, glory, Allelulia,
Glory, glory, Allelulia,
Glory, glory, Allelulia,
And we all went marching home.

44. CRESOL (The famous Army disinfectant).
TUNE: "*John Brown's Body.*"

Oh, we'll sprinkle them with Cresol,
Oh, we'll sprinkle them with Cresol,
Oh, we'll sprinkle them with Cresol,
And they shall fight no more.

45. HERE WE ARE AGAIN.

TUNE: Special.

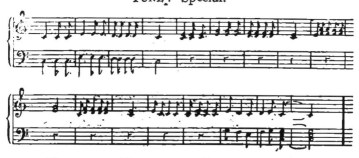

Here we are, Here we are, Here we are again,
Here we are, Here we are, Here we are again.
We beat them on the Marne,
And whacked them on the Aisne,
We smashed them up at Neuve Chapelle,
And we're ready here again.

The references to certain battle areas are too obvious to
need explanation.

46. COAL FATIGUE.

TUNE: " *Here we are, Here we are, Here we are
again.*"

Coal Fatigue, Coal Fatigue, Coal Fatigue again.
Forty tons of coal to be shifted a day

(Gawd blimey !)

Get your pick and shovel ; do it at the double ;
Are we downhearted ?—no ; let it all come.
Coal Fatigue, Coal Fatigue, Coal Fatigue again,
It'd be enough to kill Kaiser Bill.
For if you get your dinner, it's a cert you are a winner,
So Coal, Coal, Coal Fatigue again.

Coal fatigue in a big camp during winter is a very distasteful
job, especially in the mud of Salisbury Plain or the Curragh.

47. THE SOMME.

TUNE: "*Michigan.*"

I want to go back, I want to go back,
I want to go back to the Somme.
That's where I've come from
With a souvenir bit of a bomb.
I miss old Archie,
And Pont de l'Arché.
And I'll wake at 4 a.m.
I think your demoiselles are very pretty.
Nevertheless, I want to be there.
I want to hit there
A certain someone with a bomb.
That's why I wish again that I was back again,
Down on the Somme.

48. I WANT TO BE IN BLIGHTY.

TUNE: "*I want to be in Dixie.*"

I want to be—I want to be—
I want to be back home in Blighty,
From where the Huns are dog-gone glad to pour
Scrambled bombs on our butter store.
I want to be—I want to be—
I want to be back home in Blighty.
You can tell the Hun I'm going to
B.L.I.—I don't know how to spell it,
But yet I'm going—Oh! yes, I'm going
To dear old Blighty land.

49. HOO HA—HOO HA HA!

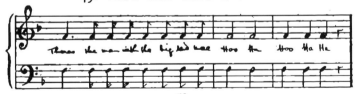

There the man with the big red nose Hoo Ha Hoo Ha Ha

50. GUILLEMONT.

TUNE: *"Moonlight Bay."*

We were rushing along
    In Guilleymong ;
We could hear the Boche a singing :
    They seemed to say,
" You have stolen our trench,
    But don't go away,
And we'll pepper you with tear shells
    All the day."

We were waiting for them
    Later on in the day ;
You might have heard our voices singing :
    " Don't lose your way.
This is your old trench,
    Now, do step this way,
And we'll give you souvenirs
    To take away."

51. I'M SO BAD.

TUNE: *" I'm in Love."*—Clarice Mayne.

Sung by troops crossing for the first or subsequent times,
especially from Southampton, with anything more than a
moderate channel swell.

I'm so bad ; I'm so bad,
You can tell by the look in my eye ;
I feel sick, oh—so sick !
I'm sure I'm just going to die, oh—my !
I've just spewed ; all my food's
Gone West,* out into the sea ;
Oh ! don't touch me yet, for I ne'er will forget
The Kaiser and his blasted army.

* A war expression meaning lost, destroyed, or killed—
presumably because the Boche fires at our troops from East to
West.

52. I WANT TO GO HOME.

TUNE: "*I want to go. Home.*"

I want to go home,
I want to go home.
I don't want to go to the trenches no more,
Where there are shells and Jack Johnsons * galore.
I want to go home,
Where the Allemand † can't get at me.
Oh my ! I don't want to die,
I want to go home.

* A 12-in. shell, or one of another big calibre.
† German.

53. OLD SOLDIERS NEVER DIE.

TUNE: "*Kind Words can Never Die.*"

Old soldiers never die, never die, never die,
Old soldiers never die, they always fade away.

54. ALSO :

This rain will never stop, never stop, never stop,
This rain will never stop—No, no, no, no, no.

Whilst on campaign, as in the sheltered days at home, the
weather can form a frequent subject as a " grouse."

55. IF IT'S A GERMAN—GUNS UP !

TUNE : " *If It's a Lady—Thumbs Up !* "

If it's a German—Guns Up !
If it's a German with hands up,
Don't start taking prisoners now,
Give it 'em in the neck and say " Bow-wow."
If it's a German—Guns Up !
Stick him in the leg—it is sublime.
If he whispers in your ear,
" Kamerad ! Kamerad ! "
Guns Up—every time.

56. ONWARD, QUEEN VICTORIAS !

TUNE : " *Onward, Christian Soldiers.*"

Onward ! Queen Victorias,
Guarding the railway line.
Is this " foreign service " ?
Ain't it jolly fine ?
No ! we're not downhearted.
Won't the Huns look sick ?
When they meet us over there,
All looking span and spick ?
Hope on, Queen Victorias !
Don't forget the fray.
We shall do our duty
For a bob a day.

57. OUR JAM.

TUNE : " *Marching through Georgia.*"

The jam, the jam, the glorious gooseberry jam,
The jam, the jam, the jam that was made for me,
The jam we spread on somebody's bed or on half a loaf
of bread,
The jam that feeds a hungry mob like we.

58. THE OLD MAN'S HAMMER.

TUNE: *"Oh! see me dance the Polka."*

Take the old man back his hammer,
'Twas a cowardly thing to do,
To take the old man's hammer
When it didn't belong to you.

So take him back his hammer,
'Twas a terrible thing to do.
You wouldn't like it if he would come
And take a hammer from you.

59. SAME TUNE:

Oh! we cannot do the Goose Step,
Oh! we will not do the Goose Step,
Oh! we shall not do the Goose Step,
Then Kaiser Bill'll go bust.

60. LEFT! LEFT!

61. WHO KILLED COCK ROBIN?

(R.F.C. Version.)

Who killed Cock Robin?
" I," said the Hun,
" With my Lewis gun,*
I killed Cock Robin."

All the planes in the air
Went a-dipping and a-throbbing,
When they heard of the death of poor Cock Robin,
When they heard of the death of poor Cock Robin.

Who saw him hit?
" I," said old Fritz,
" And I have a bit,
I saw him hit."

And all the planes in the air
Went a-swaying and a-bobbing,
When they heard of the death of poor Cock Robin,
When they heard of the death of poor Cock Robin.

Who saw him die?
" I," said the spy,
" With my telepathic eye,
I saw him die."

And all the planes in the air
Went a-strafing and a-bombing,
When they heard of the death of poor Cock Robin,
When they heard of the death of poor Cock Robin.

* Lewis gun is a machine gun fitted to aeroplanes—fires 600 round a minute.

The actions portrayed in the second line of each chorus are obvious.

62. THE ROSARY—HOSPITAL VERSION.

(*To* NURSE MORRIS, No. 2 R.C. Hospital, Rouen.)

The hours you've tended me, dear nurse,
Are as a string of pearls to me ;
I count your hours off duty with a heavy heart,
But I'm resigned—I've got to be.

Some Nurses are—and some are not.
Some Nurses can—and some cannot.
But you're one of those that are and can ;
You're an awfu' good sport—maid to man.

And when the war is over,
You'll go back to Angleterre,
You'll hear La Belle France call you—Oh ! won't
    you curse,
Mais je ne pense pas—'Twill be me, dear nurse

63. THE PILOT'S PSALM.

PARODY ON THE 23RD PSALM OF DAVID.

The BE 2c is my bus ; therefore shall I want.

He maketh me to come down in green pastures.

He leadeth me where I will not go.

He maketh me to be sick ; he leadeth me astray on all cross-country flights.

Yea : though I fly o'er No-man's land where mine enemies wouldst compass me about, I fear much evil : for *thou* art with me ; thy joystick and thy prop discomfort me.

Thou preparest a crash before me in the presence of mine enemies ; thy R.A.F. anointest my hair with oil, thy tank leaketh badly.

Surely to goodness thou shalt not follow me all the days of my life : else I shall dwell in the House at Colney Hatch for ever.

64. THE MECHANIC'S MOAN.
TUNE : " *The Rosary.*"

The hours I spent with thee, dear bus,
Are as a string of plugs to me ;
I count the clearances in all your valves,
But you will miss—and still you miss.

Some pilots are—and some are not.
Some pilots can—and some cannot.
The engine's misfiring ! now we're o'er the line ;
I'm coming back : the fault's not mine.

And when the war is over,
I'm going back to Angleterre,
And then you'll hear La Belle France calling me,
I don't think : *Je ne pense pas.*

65. THE MOUNTAINS OF MORNE.
(ANOTHER MOAN.)

Dear, mother I'm writing this letter you see ;
I'm a second A.M. in the R.F.C.,
And when I enlisted, a pilot to be ;
But oh ! 'tis never a bit of the flying I see.
The sergeant-majors, they bawl and they shout,
They don't never know what they're talking about.
Now if things don't alter I'll blooming soon be
Where the Mountains of Morne sweep down by the sea.

66. OFFICERS' WIVES.'

63

Variation for second verse.

THE RAGTIME FLYING CORPS.

TUNE : Special.

We are the Ragtime Flying Corps,
We are the ragtime boys,
We are respected by every nation
And we're loved by all the girls, I don't think.
People, they think we're millionaires,
Think we're dealers in stocks and shares ;
When we go out all the people roar,
We are the Ragtime Flying Corps.

We are the Ragtime Flying Corps,
We are the R.F.C.
We spend our tanners, we know our manners,
And are respected wherever we go.
Walking up and down the Farnborough Road,
Doors and windows open wide.
We are the boys of the R.F.C. ;
We don't care a damn for Germany ;
We are the Flying Corps.

68. THE BIRDMAN.

TUNE : " *I want to be an Angel.*"

I want to be an airman bold,
To mingle with the stars,
To fly all weathers, hot and cold,
To be a son of Mars.
I fear no Hun ; no, far or near,
While my gun's mounted in the rear,
And I've a Vickers* by my side,
To be my escort and my guide.

---

* A machine-gun—now much in favour as a fixed gun to fire
between the propeller blades.

69. THE RAGTIME AIRCRAFT BUILDERS.

Tune : " *Here we go gathering Nuts and May.*"

This they call a factory,
                a factory,
                a factory.
Its breadth and width is three by three,
It's called the R.A.F.*

And here we build our aeroplanes,
                        a biplane,
                        and a monoplane.
With silly work we're nigh insane,
At the factory for aircraft.

Now two big sheets† from mother's bed,
                        not sister's bed,
                        nor Lucy's bed.
Two big sheets from mother's bed,
They'll come in very handy.

Two big wheels from father's car,
                    father's car,
                    father's car.
Two big wheels‡ from father's car,
They'll do very well.

Now this they call a fuselage,§
                    a fuselage,
                    not mucilage.
You only call it fuselage
When you're in the know.

Next we have the longeron,‖
   the longeron,
    the one plus long.
Now that we have a longeron,
We'll stick it in the middle.
Now we'll shove the joystick in,¶
    joystick in,
    joystick in.
We'll just shove the joystick in
To make it look complete.

Next we'll have the motoro,**
   the R.A.F.,
  which will not go.
It's quite a puzzle to those in the know,
With all its idiosyncrasies.

We mustn't forget the old windstick,††
   it goes all right
   without a flick.
But sometimes stops—then we look sick→
At five o'clock in the morning.

And now we've made an aeroplane,
   Is't a biplane
   Or monoplane ?
We'll pack it up and send it by train,
So as not to spoil it.

   (*Over the lines.*)
I think they're off their beastly rocker,
   perhaps they think
   it's a game of soccer.
They send me out against a Fokker :‡‡
They must have lost their valve-head.

(*Two months later*.)

And here I am in hospital,

in hospital,

Far from Pall Mall.

But when I come out, I shall resign

My commission in the Army.

* Pronounced **Arayeff** in this case, usually pronounced as spelt—" **raf** " ; stands for the Government-owned Royal Aircraft Factory at Farnboro', Hants.

† In lieu of fabric.

‡ For the landing chassis.

§ The portion of an aeroplane connecting the planes with the tail.

‖ The main longitudinal members, usually of wood, on which the fuselage is built up.

¶ Control lever, sometimes known as the *cloche.*

** A R.A.F. production of ill repute.

†† The propeller, usually known nowadays as the " prop."

‡‡ Written at the time of the Fokker scourge—when BE 2 c's were being beaten wholesale.

70. THE MECHANICS' ROSARY.

(R.F.C. PARODY.)

TUNE : " *My Mother's Rosary.*"

There's an awful noise at times

Comes from out our planes.

Jim—'e calls it 'orrid names,

Says it gives 'im pains

Without any rhyme,

Without any prose.

One can never get the blamed thing to go ;

But ten great big cylinders,

And ten great big valves :

You'll take them out,

You'll put them in,

And when your daily work is done,

You'll count them each and every one—

That is *your* Rosary.

71. OH, YOU BEAUTIFUL BUS !*

TUNE : " *Oh, you beautiful Doll !* "

(R.F.C. PARODY.)

Oh, you beautiful bus !
You great big beautiful bus !
Let me take the wireless off you,
Put the blooming bomb racks on you.
Oh, you beautiful bus !
You great big beautiful bus !
If I should ever leave you, oh, my heart would ache ;
I would hug you, but I fear you'd break,
Oh, oh, oh, oh, oh, you beautiful bus !

* Pet name for all aeroplanes. Aviators, like yachtsmen
never allude to their craft as aeroplanes.

72. YOU'RE SOME AEROPLANE.

TUNE : " *Beautiful Baby Doll.*"

(R.F.C. PARODY.)

You're some aeroplane,
You're at your tricks again.
When you start that flying,
It's a style of your own.
I can't help but holler out, " Good-bye, happy home."
Oh ! Oh ! hold on tight,
It's going to loop with all its might.
Oh ! when you dip, as you always do,
I have nothing at all to do.
Oh ! I can feel you strain,
You horrible aeroplane !

73. ODE TO THE R.A.F. (Engine).

Eight little cylinders sitting facing heaven,
One blew its head off—then there were seven.
Seven little cylinders used to playing tricks,
One warped its inlet valve—then there were six.
Six little cylinders working all alive,
One got a sooted plug—then there were five.
Five little cylinders working all the more,
One overworked itself—then there were four.
Four little cylinders flying o'er the sea,
One shed a piston ring—then there were three.
Three little cylinders wondering what to do,
One over-oiled itself—then there were two.
Two little cylinders very nearly done,
One broke a valve stem—then there was one.
One little cylinder trying to pull round seven,
    At length gave its efforts up and ascended into
        heaven.

74. GREENER GROWS THE GRASS.

TUNE : See Ode to R.A.F., page 70.

Higher up the mountain,
Greener grows the grass :
Down came an elephant
Sliding on a threepenny bit.
Five-and-twenty navvies
Working on a line :
Five-and-twenty bob a week
And all the overtime.

Higher up the mountain,
Greener grows the grass.
The more the donkey wags his tail,
The more you see his
Ask a policeman :
Hear him say you nay ;
Morning, noon, and night-time—
Ask him all the day.

75. NAPOO—FINI ! ! !*

TUNE : " *Keep the Home Fires burning.*"
(R.F.C. PARODY.)

Keep the 2 c's burning,†
Watch the windsticks squirming,
The R.A.F. has chugged his inside out,
All on his blooming own.
Can't yer 'ear it grinding ?
'Oo the 'ell's a-pining ?
Don't yer 'ear the fabric rip ?—
List ter its sad, sad moan !

* Tommy's contraction of " *Il n'y-a plus* " : means finished ;
no more ; lost ; forgotten, etc.
† BE 2c—a machine of Government design meant to be a
general utility machine ; *see* other references.

76. RECRUITING SONG R.F.C. No. 1.
SPECIAL TUNE.

I was standing at the corner,
When I heard somebody say :
" Come to join the Flying Corps,
Come, step along, this way."
I threw my thirty* chest out,
And put my cap on straight,
And walked into the office
Along with Jack, my mate.

They offered me two bob a day,†
I said, " I didn't think,"
But when they murmured, " Four bob,"‡
I said, " Come, have a drink."
And now I spend my Sundays
With Lizzie in the Lane.
I wonder when I'll get my " first "§
Or see an aeroplane.

I never was so well off
In all my naturel :
You should see me in St. James's,
I am an awful swell.
And now I've been to Larkhill,‖
My education is complete.
" Form fours," " 'Bout turn," " Two deep,"
Oh ! don't I do it neat.

You should see us hold our heads up
When the others pass us by.
The girls they all run after us
And, breathless, say, " Oh my !
Dear Tommy brave, I'll be your slave,
If you will take me up."
But hastily I answer,
" I've an invitation out to sup."

77. RECRUITING SONG R.F.C. No. 2.

TUNE : " *The Lowther Arcade and The Tin Gee-Gee.*"

I was walking in town up Regent Street
    When I saw the R.F.C.
I thought to myself—Now, they look neat—
    I think that would suit me.
So I strolled inside, and carefully lied
    About my carpentry,*
But when I came out, I swaggered about—
    For I was in the R.F.C.

They sent me down to Salisbury Plain
    To a place they call Larkhill.
The sergeants they bullied with might and main
    And made us do some drill.
All the fellows they were " risky," they smoked naught
        but De Reske
    When going to the Y.M. hut.
And they didn't do us badly—tho' we weren't from Pope
        and Bradley—†
    For we were the Flying Corps—Tut ! Tut !

76. RECRUITING SONG R.F.C. No 1.

* 30 inches.
† Pay of second class air mechanic.
‡ Pay of first-class air mechanic.
§ To get one's " first " is to be promoted from 2/A.M. to 1/A.M.
‖ One-time training ground for drill, etc., for the R.F.C.
    It is interesting to record here that air mechanics are invariably referred to as " ackemmas "—*i.e.*, 1st ackemma or 2nd ackemma—this being the Army signal way of distinguishing letters when words are spelt over the 'phone.

77. RECRUITING SONG R.F.C. No 2.

    * The writer has personal knowledge of an " air mechanic " who was enlisted as a carpenter and knew not one wood and scarcely one tool from another. Such incidents were frequent —trade tests being very superficial and the testers presumably open to bribes.
    †¡One of the earliest tailoring firms to specialise in R.F.C. tunics, or " maternity jackets "—as they are popularly known.

78. "EXCELSIOR" UP TO DATE.

The shades of night were falling fast
As to the aerodrome there passed
A youth, with jaw set like a vice,
Who bore aloft this strange device :
KEEP FLYING !

His brow was glad ; his eyes were bright,
Reflected in the starry night !
And as he staggered to his bus,
We heard him faintly whisper thus :
KEEP FLYING !

" Beware the Lewis gun that jambs !
Beware the shaky struts and cams !
The engine, too, is thick with rust."
" Oh, rats ! " the youth replied. " I must
KEEP FLYING ! "

" Try not the flight ! " the sergeant pressed.
" 'Twill mean ' No flowers, by request,'
And currents roll both deep and wide ! "
But loud that clarion voice replied :
" KEEP FLYING ! "

" Oh, stay ! " the Flight Commander said,
" The wine in mess flows good and red,
The sherry sparkles, rich and bright ! "
A voice replied, far up the height :
" KEEP FLYING ! "

At break of day we started out
And scanned the heavens for his Scout.
And as we whistled through the air
We heard a dulcet voice declare :
" KEEP FLYING ! "

There, in the tree-top, that young coon
Perched like a punctured kite balloon.
And when the ambulance drew nigh
We heard his last despairing cry :
　　　　　　" Keep Flying ! "

　　　　　　　　　　G. R. S.
Aeronautics, 29-8-'17.

79. LOOPING THE LOOP.
Tune : Special.

Looping the loop with Lucy Loo,
Looping the loop with Lu ;
Whirling and twirling the whole day long.
In a bus that's built for two ;
Then up in the sky so high we fly,
And then with a rush we go.
It's just the same motion
You get on the ocean
That you're forced to say " 'Arf a mo "

80. THE DYING AVIATOR.

Tune: "*The Dying Lancer.*"

Solo.

A handsome young airman lay dying,

(chorus) : *lay dying,*

And as on the aer'drome he lay,

he lay,

To the mechanics who round him came sighing,

came sighing,

These last dying words he did say,

he did say :

" Take the cylinder out of my kidneys,"

" *of his kidneys,*"

" The connecting rod out of my brain,"

" *of his brain,*"

" The cam box from under my backbone,"

" *his backbone,*"

" And assemble the engine again,"

" *again.*"

81. OH, HAD I THE WINGS OF AN AVRO!

Tune: "*The Dying Lancer.*"

Solo.

Oh, had I the wings of an Avro,

(chorus) : " *of an Avro,*"

Then, far, far away I would soar,

" *would soar,*"

Right off to my pals down in Holland,

" *in Holland,*"

And rest there the rest of the war,

" *the war.*"

82. ESPRIT DE CORPS.

(An Authenticated Epic.)

Tune : " *The Dying Lancer*."
Solo.

Wrap me up in my old yellow jacket,
  The one in which I used to soar ;

     (chorus) : *to soar* ;

Give my helmet, my map and my goggles—
  I feel once again as of yore.

     as of yore.

Fasten the jacket around me,
  Lift me into my place ;

     my place ;

For ne'er shall ye say I'd the wind up,
  I've still life enough for the pace.

     for the pace.

Wrap me up in my old yellow jacket,
  Give met the joystick to hold ;

     to hold ;

Let me fly once again o'er the trench line—
  Thus shall my exploits be told.

     be told.

Oh ! it's good to be in the old jacket,
  To hear, " Switch off—petrol on, sir " ;

     " *petrol on* " ;

To repeat once again the word " contact,"
  To hear the old engine go whir-r-r-r.

     go whir-r-r-r.

Now we're off—o'er the line will we *allez*,
  To strafe and to bomb is our aim ;

     our aim ;

To win or to lose in a combat—
  The game must be played just the same.

     just the same.

Ah ! see that Hun there—in the sun, lad,
    Give him a burst of the best :
                              of the best :
Poop, poop, poop—he's returning our fire.
I must splitass and stunt round him, lest . . .
                            round him, lest . . .

God ! I'm hit, curse him—I feel so dizzy ;
    I'm sorry, old thing—it's my fault ;
                            my fault ;
My hand or my eyes not so steady :
    I don't feel as well as I thought.
                          as I thought.

     . . . .

Down, down, in a nose-dive they're spinning,
    Down from ten thousand to two :
                            to two :
Very slowly the machine comes out level,
    The sands of life not yet run thro'.
                          not run through.

By instinct his actions are guided,
    The machine flying homeward bound now :
                            bound now ;
Th' observer, a-sweat and a-tremble,
    Scarce knows what has happened—nor how.
                          nor how.

He knows naught of the art of controlling
    An unstable bus in the air ;
                            in the air ;
It's his first ascent into the heavens—
    Sure, 'tis an experience rare.
                          very rare.

Dazed—yet alive—he is landing :
   Blood from his scalp surges down ;
                      from his crown ;
He moves not as they rush towards him,
   Ere then—his brave spirit has flown.
                      has flown.

      .   .   .   .

They laid him in his old yellow jacket,
   In peace ; and his spirit may soar
                      may soar
Far above, where the Huns cease from troubling,
   And Lewis guns rattle no more.
                      no more.

83.   A STRAFE ON THE KAISER.
TUNE : Special.

We haven't seen the Kaiser for a hell of a time,
      Hell of a time—Hell of a time.
We came to France to see what he was doing,
The Royal Flying Corps will be his ruddy ruin :
Oh, we haven't seen the Kaiser for a hell of a time,
He must have been a-blown up by a mine.
For he's the leader of the German band.
Gott strafe him, he's a cousin of mine.

84.   WHEN THEY WERE UP, THEY WERE UP.

The brave old Duke of York,
He had ten thousand men :
He marched them up to the top of the hill,
And marched them down again.
      And when they were up, they were up,
      And when they were down, they were down,
      But when they were halfway up that hill,
      They were neither up nor down.

85. THE GREEN GRASS GREW ALL ROUND.

Tune : Special.

For there was a little mill,
And the mill was on the hill,
And the hill stood still,
And the green grass grew all round ;
And the green grass grew all around, my boys,
The green grass grew all round.

For there was a little tree,
And the tree was near the mill,
And the mill was on the hill,
And the hill stood still,
And the green grass grew all round ;
And the green grass grew all around, my boys,
The green grass grew all round.

For there was a little bough
That grew upon the tree,
And the tree was near the mill,
And the mill was on the hill,
And the hill stood still,
And the green grass grew all round ;
And the green grass grew all around, my boys,
The green grass grew all round.

For there was a little branch,
And the branch was on the bough,

And the bough was on the tree,
And the tree was near the mill,
And the mill was on the hill,
And the hill stood still,
And the green grass grew all round ;
And the green grass grew all around, my boys,
The green grass grew all round.

For there came a little bird,
Who sat upon that branch,
And the branch was on the bough,
And the bough was on the tree,
And the tree was near the mill,
And the mill was on the hill,
And the hill stood still,
And the green grass grew all round ;
And the green grass grew all around, my boys,
The green grass grew all round.

WITH EXTENSIONS *ad infinitum.*

86. THE SEAFORTH'S SOB.

TUNE : " *Yankee Doodle.*"

You may have fought the Turk, sir,
    And think it very funny
That tho' the Seaforths do the work,
    The Sappers get the money.

87. NO QUARTER.

TUNE : " *Yankee Doodle.*"

Kaiser Bill, he went to war
Athirst for blood and slaughter :
He lost his crown—so he feels sore ;
And so he bally well oughter.

88. DOWN IN THE VALLEY.

TUNE : Special.

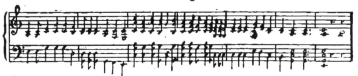

The first time I met her she was dressed all in green,
    All in green,
    All in green.
    Prettiest girl I've ever seen,
Down in the valley where she followed me.

The next time I met her she was dressed all in grey,
    All in grey,
    All in grey.
    Oh ! I'll ne'er forget that day
Down in the valley where she followed me.

The third time I met her she was dressed all in mauve,
    All in mauve,
    All in mauve.
    Guess how my eyes did rove
Down in the valley where she followed me.

The next time I met her she was dressed all in pink,
    All in pink,
    All in pink.
    Took her to the open air rink
Down in the valley where she followed me.

The next time I met her she was dressed all in brown,
    All in brown,
    All in brown.
    On the grass did we sit down,
Down in the valley where she followed me.

The next time I met her she was dressed all in blue,
>All in blue,
>All in blue.
>You should have seen us bill and coo
Down in the valley where she followed me.

The next time I met her she was dressed all in white,
>All in white,
>All in white.
>My !—I had an awful night
Down in the valley where she followed me.

The next time I met her she was dressed all in yellow,
>All in yellow,
>All in yellow.
>Kissed by some other fellow
Down in the valley where she followed me.

The next time I met her she was dressed all in scarlet,
>All in scarlet,
>All in scarlet,
>Just like a common harlot,
Down in the valley where she followed me.

The next time I met her she was dressed all in red,
>All in red,
>All in red.
>Two little kiddies dead,
Down in the valley where she followed me.

The last time I met her she was dressed all in black,
>All in black,
>All in black.
>Out on the other fellow's track,
Down in the valley where she followed me.

TUNE FOR LAST VERSE : " *Farmer Giles.*"
Now this is the moral to all those who think :
Don't take a strange girl to an open-air rink ;
Don't sit on the grass, as I've already said,
Or may all your troubles be on your own head.

83

89. OHIO.

TUNE : Special.

Old Macdougal had a farm in Ohio-i-o,
And on that farm he had some dogs in Ohio-i-o.
With a bow-wow here, and a bow-wow there,
Here a bow, there a wow, everywhere a bow-wow.

Old Macdougal had a farm in Ohio-i-o,
And on that farm he had some hens in Ohio-i-o.
With a cluck cluck here, and a cluck cluck there,
Here a cluck, there a cluck, everywhere a cluck, cluck.

Old Macdougal had a farm in Ohio-i-o,
And on that farm he had some ducks in Ohio-i-o.
With a quack quack here, and a quack quack there,
Here a quack, there a quack, everywhere a quack, quack.

Old Macdougal had a farm in Ohio-i-o,
And on that farm he had some cows in Ohio-i-o.
With a moo moo here, and a moo moo there,
Here a moo, there a moo, everywhere a moo moo.

Old Macdougal had a farm in Ohio-i-o,
And on that farm he had some pigs in Ohio-i-o.
With a grunt grunt here, and a grunt grunt there,
Here a grunt, there a grunt, everywhere a grunt grunt.

Old Macdougal had a farm in Ohio-i-o,
And on that farm he had some cats in Ohio-i-o.
With a meow meow here, and a meow meow there,
Here a meow, there a meow, everywhere a meow meow.

Old Macdougal had a farm in Ohio-i-o,
And on that farm he had an ass in Ohio-i-o.
With a hee-haw here, and a hee-haw there,
Here a hee, there a haw, everywhere a hee-haw.
Meow-meow, grunt-grunt, moo-moo, quack-quack,
Cluck-cluck, bow-wow.
Old Macdougal had a farm in Ohio-i-o.

90. WE ARE THE BOYS WHO MAKE NO NOISE.

Tune : Special.

We are the boys that make no noise,
Although we're out in France.
We are the boys that make no noise,
We lead the Huns a dance.
We are the heroes of the night,
But we'd rather eat than fight.
We are the heroes of the gallant Fusiliers.

The references to feeding in all these songs are prolific.

91. THE MAN, THE DOG AND THE MEADOW.
TUNE : Special.

One man went to mow,
    Went to mow a meadow.
One man and his dawg
    Went to mow a meadow.

Two men went to mow,
    Went to mow a meadow.
Two men, one man (and his dawg)
    Went to mow a meadow.

Three men went to mow,
    Went to mow a meadow,
Three men, two men, one man (and his dawg)
    Went to mow a meadow.

Four men went to mow,
    Went to mow a meadow.
Four men, three men, two men, one man (and his dawg)
    Went to mow a meadow.

Five men went to mow,
    Went to mow a meadow.
Five men, four men, three men, two men, one man (and
      his dawg)
    Went to mow a meadow.

Six men went to mow,
    Went to mow a meadow.
Six men, five men, four men, three men, two men, one
      man (and his dawg)
    Went to mow a meadow.

Seven men went to mow,
    Went to mow a meadow.
Seven men, six men, five men, four men, three men, two
      men, one man (and his dawg)
    Went to mow a meadow.

Eight men went to mow,
    Went to mow a meadow.
Eight men, seven men, six men, five men, four men,
      three men, two men, one man (and his dawg)
    Went to mow a meadow.

Nine men went to mow,
    Went to mow a meadow.
Nine men, eight men, seven men, six men, five men, four
      men, three men, two men, one man (and his dawg)
    Went to mow a meadow.

Ten men went to mow,
    Went to mow a meadow.
Ten men, nine men, eight men, seven men, six men, five
      men, four men, three men, two men, one man (and
      his dawg)
    NEVER mowed that meadow.
              AND SO ON, until out of breath.

92. CALL THE ROLL ! ! !
TUNE : Special.

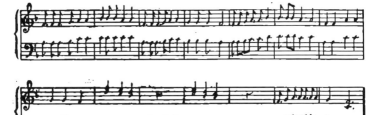

Early in the morning, down at the station,
See the little puff-puffs all in a row ;
Man at the engine turns a little handle :
Choo ! choo ! choo ! choo ! off they go.

Call the roll, call the roll, call the roll, call the roll,
  And we'll meet you at the cookhouse door.

Early in the morning, on the parade ground,
See the little fatigews* all in a row ;
Up comes the sergeant, gives them their orders :
Left, right ! left, right ! off they go.

  Call the roll, call the roll, call the roll, call the roll,
    And we'll meet you at the cookhouse door.

Early in the morning, outside the sick tent,
See the little sick boys all in a row ;
Up comes the Doctor, gives them each a No. 9 :†
Left, right ! left, right ! off they go.

  Call the roll, call the roll, call the roll, call the roll,
    And we'll meet you at the lathouse door.‡

* Men detailed for fatigue or routine drudgery.
† A pill ; an aperient.
‡ Latrines.

93. NINETY-NINE BOTTLES ON THE WALL.

There were ninety-nine bottles hanging on the wall,
There were ninety-nine bottles hanging on the wall.
What would happen if one were to fall?
Why, there'd be ninety-eight bottles hanging on the wall

There were ninety-eight bottles hanging on the wall,
There were ninety-eight bottles hanging on the wall.
Oh, what would happen were another to fall?
Why, there'd still be ninety-seven bottles hanging on
the wall.

Ninety-seven bottles hanging on the wall,
Ninety-seven bottles hanging on the wall.
What would happen if another were to fall?
Why, there'd still be ninety-six bottles hanging on that
wall.

Ninety-six bottles hanging on the wall,
Ninety-six bottles hanging on the wall.
Oh, nothing would happen were another to fall,
'Cos there'd still be ninety-five bottles hanging on that
wall.

AND SO ON, until tired.

94. RONNEL McCONNEL.*

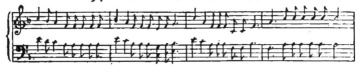

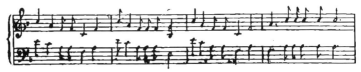

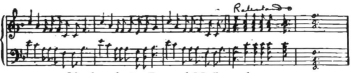

Oh, here's to Ronnel McConnel,
Oh, here's to a bottle of beer,
Oh, here's to Ronnel McConnel—
We're all good company here.
So put your left leg out,*
An' pull your right leg in,*
An' gie yersel's a shake,*
An' turn yersel's about.*

Oh, here's to Ronnel McConnel,
Oh, here's to a bottle of beer,
Oh, here's to Ronnel McConnel,
We're all good company HERE.

* This should be sung standing, and action should be suited
to the words as described.

95. BOYS' BRIGADE.
TUNE: " *Bugle Call.*"
Here comes the Boys' Brigade,
All smothered in marmalade,
A tuppeny ha'penny pillpot,
And half a yard of braid.

96. WHITER THAN THE WHITEWASH.

I shall be whiter than the whitewash on the wall,
I shall be whiter than the whitewash on the wall.
Wash me in the water that you wash your dirty daughter
in,
And I shall be whiter than the whitewash on the wall.

Chorus :

  Whiter than the wall,
  Whiter than the wall ;
Oh ! wash me in the water that you wash your dirty
daughter in,
And I shall be whiter than the whitewash on the wall.

97. 1815—1915.

Tune : *" British Grenadiers."*

There was a brave old Scotchie
At the Battle of Waterloo ;
The wind blew up his kilties,
And he didn't know what to do.